ABOUT KUMON

KUM☺N®
MATH. READING. SUCCESS.

What is Kumon?

Kumon is the world's largest supplemental education provider and a leader in producing outstanding results. After-school programs in math and reading at Kumon Centers around the globe have been helping children succeed for 50 years.

Kumon Workbooks represent just a fraction of our complete curriculum of preschool-to-college-level material assigned at Kumon Centers under the supervision of trained Kumon Instructors.

The Kumon Method enables each child to progress successfully by practicing material until concepts are mastered and advancing in small, manageable increments. Instructors carefully assign materials and pace advancement according to the strengths and needs of each individual student.

Students usually attend a Kumon Center twice a week and practice at home the other five days. Assignments take about twenty minutes.

Kumon helps students of all ages and abilities master the basics, improve concentration and study habits, and build confidence.

How did Kumon begin?

IT ALL BEGAN IN JAPAN 50 YEARS AGO when a parent and teacher named Toru Kumon found a way to help his son Takeshi do better in school. At the prompting of his wife, he created a series of short assignments that his son could complete successfully in less than 20 minutes a day and that would ultimately make high school math easy. Because each was just a bit more challenging than the last, Takeshi was able to master the skills and gain the confidence to keep advancing.

This unique self-learning method was so successful that Toru's son was able to do calculus by the time he was in the sixth grade. Understanding the value of good reading comprehension, Mr. Kumon then developed a reading program employing the same method. His programs are the basis and inspiration of those offered at Kumon Centers today under the expert guidance of professional Kumon Instructors.

Mr. Toru Kumon
Founder of Kumon

What can Kumon do for my child?

Kumon is geared to children of all ages and skill levels. Whether you want to give your child a leg up in his or her schooling, build a strong foundation for future studies or address a possible learning problem, Kumon provides an effective program for developing key learning skills given the strengths and needs of each individual child.

What makes Kumon so different?

Kumon uses neither a classroom model nor a tutoring approach. It's designed to facilitate self-acquisition of the skills and study habits needed to improve academic performance. This empowers children to succeed on their own, giving them a sense of accomplishment that fosters further achievement. Whether for remedial work or enrichment, a child advances according to individual ability and initiative to reach his or her full potential. Kumon is not only effective, but also surprisingly affordable.

What is the role of the Kumon Instructor?

Kumon Instructors regard themselves more as mentors or coaches than teachers in the traditional sense. Their principal role is to provide the direction, support and encouragement that will guide the student to performing at 100% of his or her potential. Along with their rigorous training in the Kumon Method, all Kumon Instructors share a passion for education and an earnest desire to help children succeed.

KUMON FOSTERS:

- A mastery of the basics of reading and math
- Improved concentration and study habits
- Increased self-discipline and self-confidence
- A proficiency in material at every level
- Performance to each student's full potential
- A sense of accomplishment

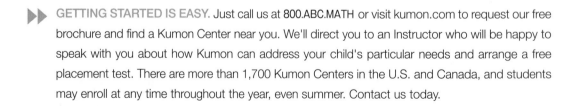

GETTING STARTED IS EASY. Just call us at 800.ABC.MATH or visit kumon.com to request our free brochure and find a Kumon Center near you. We'll direct you to an Instructor who will be happy to speak with you about how Kumon can address your child's particular needs and arrange a free placement test. There are more than 1,700 Kumon Centers in the U.S. and Canada, and students may enroll at any time throughout the year, even summer. Contact us today.

Name
Date

To parents

Your child will first review the numbers 1-50. If he or she is having difficulty with this section, try some extended practice with numbers before continuing.

■ Say each number aloud as you trace it.

1	2	3	4	5	6	7	8	9	10
1	2	3	4	5	6	7	8	9	10

11	12	13	14	15	16	17	18	19	20
11	12	13	14	15	16	17	18	19	20

21	22	23	24	25	26	27	28	29	30
21	22	23	24	25	26	27	28	29	30

31	32	33	34	35	36	37	38	39	40
31	32	33	34	35	36	37	38	39	40

41	42	43	44	45	46	47	48	49	50
41	42	43	44	45	46	47	48	49	50

■ Say each number aloud as you trace or write it.

1	2	3	4	5	6	7	8	9	10
1									10

11	12	13	14	15	16	17	18	19	20
11									20

21	22	23	24	25	26	27	28	29	30
21									30

31	32	33	34	35	36	37	38	39	40
31									40

41	42	43	44	45	46	47	48	49	50
41									50

Name

Date

To parents
Your child will now review some simple addition, which will help him or
her transition to simple multiplication.

■ Add the numbers below.

(1) $1 + 1 =$ 2

(2) $2 + 1 =$ 3

(3) $3 + 1 =$ 4

(4) $4 + 1 =$ 5

(5) $5 + 1 =$ 6

(6) $6 + 1 =$ 7

(7) $7 + 1 =$ 8

(8) $8 + 1 =$ 9

(9) $9 + 1 =$ 10

(10) $1 + 2 =$ 3

(11) $2 + 2 =$ 4

(12) $3 + 2 =$ 5

(13) $4 + 2 =$ 6

(14) $5 + 2 =$ 7

(15) $6 + 2 =$ 8

(16) $7 + 2 =$ 9

(17) $8 + 2 =$ 10

(18) $9 + 2 =$ 11

(19) $1 + 3 =$

(20) $2 + 3 =$ 5

3+3 to 4+5

■ Add the numbers below.

(1) 3 + 3 = 6

(2) 4 + 3 = 7

(3) 5 + 3 = 8

(4) 6 + 3 = 9

(5) 7 + 3 = 10

(6) 8 + 3 = 11

(7) 9 + 3 = 12

(8) 1 + 4 = 5

(9) 2 + 4 = 6

(10) 3 + 4 = 7

(11) 4 + 4 = 8

(12) 5 + 4 = 9

(13) 6 + 4 = 10

(14) 7 + 4 = 11

(15) 8 + 4 = 12

(16) 9 + 4 = 13

(17) 1 + 5 = 6

(18) 2 + 5 = 7

(19) 3 + 5 = 8

(20) 4 + 5 = 9

Practicing Addition

1+1 to 9+5

Name

Date

■ Add the numbers below.

(1) $5 + 5 = 10$

(2) $6 + 5 = 11$

(3) $7 + 5 = 12$

(4) $8 + 5 = 13$

(5) $9 + 5 = 14$

(6) $8 + 4 = 12$

(7) $7 + 1 = 8$

(8) $9 + 2 = 11$

(9) $4 + 4 = 8$

(10) $2 + 3 = 5$

(11) $1 + 1 = 2$

(12) $3 + 2 = 5$

(13) $7 + 4 = 11$

(14) $3 + 3 = 6$

(15) $6 + 1 = 7$

(16) $7 + 2 = 9$

(17) $8 + 3 = 11$

(18) $9 + 4 = 13$

(19) $2 + 2 = 4$

(20) $3 + 1 = 4$

■ Add the numbers below.

(1) 5 + 5 = 10

(2) 6 + 4 = 10

(3) 8 + 3 = 11

(4) 7 + 5 = 12

(5) 1 + 1 = 3

(6) 9 + 2 = 11

(7) 4 + 5 = 9

(8) 3 + 4 = 7

(9) 5 + 3 = 8

(10) 4 + 5 = 9

(11) 2 + 2 = 4

(12) 2 + 5 = 7

(13) 7 + 4 = 11

(14) 9 + 3 = 12

(15) 8 + 5 = 13

(16) 5 + 1 = 6

(17) 6 + 4 = 10

(18) 3 + 3 = 6

(19) 4 + 4 = 8

(20) 9 + 5 = 14

Name

Date

To parents

Repeated addition is a good preparation for multiplication. In order to help your child see the link between the two, you could ask him or her how many 1s there are in each number sentence below.

■ Say each number aloud as you trace it.

1	2	3	4	5	6	7	8	9	10
11	12	13	14	15	16	17	18	19	20
21	22	23	24	25	26	27	28	29	30
31	32	33	34	35	36	37	38	39	40
41	42	43	44	45	46	47	48	49	50

1	2	3	4	5	6	7	8	9	10

(1) $1 + 1 = 2$

(2) $1 + 1 + 1 = 3$

(3) $1 + 1 + 1 + 1 = 4$

(4) $1 + 1 + 1 + 1 + 1 = 5$

(5) $1 + 1 + 1 + 1 + 1 + 1 = 6$

(6) $1 + 1 + 1 + 1 + 1 + 1 + 1 = 7$

(7) $1 + 1 + 1 + 1 + 1 + 1 + 1 + 1 = 8$

(8) $1 + 1 + 1 + 1 + 1 + 1 + 1 + 1 + 1 = 9$

(9) $1 + 1 + 1 + 1 + 1 + 1 + 1 + 1 + 1 + 1 = 10$

■ Draw a line from 1 to 10 in order while saying each number aloud.

■ Add the numbers below.

(1) | + | = 2

(2) | + | + | = 3

(3) | + | + | + | = 4

(4) | + | + | + | + | = 5

(5) | + | + | + | + | + | = 6

(6) | + | + | + | + | + | + | = 7

(7) | + | + | + | + | + | + | + | = 8

(8) | + | + | + | + | + | + | + | + | = 9

(9) | + | + | + | + | + | + | + | + | + | = 10

Name

Date

To parents

On this page, your child will practice repeated addition. This is a basic step on the road to understanding multiplication.

■ Say each number aloud as you trace it.

(1) I + I = 2

(2) I + I + I = 3

(3) I + I + I + I = 4

(4) I + I + I + I + I = 5

■ Write the numbers in the number line. Then add the numbers below.

1 2 3 4 5

(1) I + I = 2

(2) I + I + I = 3

(3) I + I + I + I = 4

(4) I + I + I + I + I = 5

6 to 10

■ Say each number aloud as you trace it.

6	7	8	9	10

(1) $| + | + | + | + | + | = $ 6

(2) $| + | + | + | + | + | + | = $ 7

(3) $| + | + | + | + | + | + | + | = $ 8

(4) $| + | + | + | + | + | + | + | + | = $ 9

(5) $| + | + | + | + | + | + | + | + | + | = $ 10

■ Write the numbers in the number line. Then add the numbers below.

6	7	8	9	10

(1) $| + | + | + | + | + | = $ 6

(2) $| + | + | + | + | + | + | = $ 7

(3) $| + | + | + | + | + | + | + | = $ 8

(4) $| + | + | + | + | + | + | + | + | = $ 9

(5) $| + | + | + | + | + | + | + | + | + | = $ 10

6 Multiplication I
1×1 to 1×10

Name

Date

To parents
From this page on, your child will practice multiplication tables for the numbers 1 through 5. If your child has difficulty understanding these number sentences, help him or her understand that 1×1 is "one group of one," for example.

■ Read the multiplication table aloud.

Multiplication Table

(1) $1 \times 1 = 1$ One times one is one.

(2) $1 \times 2 = 2$ One times two is two.

(3) $1 \times 3 = 3$ One times three is three.

(4) $1 \times 4 = 4$ One times four is four.

(5) $1 \times 5 = 5$ One times five is five.

(6) $1 \times 6 = 6$ One times six is six.

(7) $1 \times 7 = 7$ One times seven is seven.

(8) $1 \times 8 = 8$ One times eight is eight.

(9) $1 \times 9 = 9$ One times nine is nine.

(10) $1 \times 10 = 10$ One times ten is ten.

■ Read each number sentence aloud as you trace the answer.

(1) $1 \times 1 = 1$

(2) $1 \times 2 = 2$

(3) $1 \times 3 = 3$

(4) $1 \times 4 = 4$

(5) $1 \times 5 = 5$

(6) $1 \times 6 = 6$

(7) $1 \times 7 = 7$

(8) $1 \times 8 = 8$

(9) $1 \times 9 = 9$

(10) $1 \times 10 = 10$

1×1 to 1×10

■ Multiply the numbers below.

(1) $1 \times 1 = 1$

(2) $1 \times 2 = 2$

(3) $1 \times 3 = 3$

(4) $1 \times 4 = 4$

(5) $1 \times 5 = 5$

(6) $1 \times 6 = 6$

(7) $1 \times 7 = 7$

(8) $1 \times 8 = 8$

(9) $1 \times 9 = 9$

(10) $1 \times 10 = 10$

(11) $1 \times 1 = 1$

(12) $1 \times 2 = 2$

(13) $1 \times 3 = 3$

(14) $1 \times 4 = 4$

(15) $1 \times 5 = 5$

(16) $1 \times 6 = 6$

(17) $1 \times 7 = 7$

(18) $1 \times 8 = 8$

(19) $1 \times 9 = 9$

(20) $1 \times 10 = 10$

Multiplication 1

1×1 to 1×10

Name

Date

■ Multiply the numbers below.

(1) $1 \times 3 = 3$

(2) $1 \times 6 = 6$

(3) $1 \times 9 = 9$

(4) $1 \times 5 = 5$

(5) $1 \times 1 = 1$

(6) $1 \times 7 = 7$

(7) $1 \times 2 = 2$

(8) $1 \times 8 = 8$

(9) $1 \times 10 = 10$

(10) $1 \times 4 = 4$

(11) $1 \times 9 = 9$

(12) $1 \times 1 = 1$

(13) $1 \times 7 = 7$

(14) $1 \times 10 = 10$

(15) $1 \times 8 = 8$

(16) $1 \times 3 = 3$

(17) $1 \times 5 = 5$

(18) $1 \times 2 = 2$

(19) $1 \times 4 = 4$

(20) $1 \times 6 = 6$

1 × 1 to 1 × 10

■ Multiply the numbers below.

(1) 1 × 4 = 4   (11) 1 × 9 = 9

(2) 1 × 7 = 7   (12) 1 × 3 = 3

(3) 1 × 10 = 10   (13) 1 × 1 = 1

(4) 1 × 2 = 2   (14) 1 × 4 = 4

(5) 1 × 6 = 6   (15) 1 × 10 = 10

(6) 1 × 1 = 1   (16) 1 × 5 = 5

(7) 1 × 8 = 8   (17) 1 × 7 = 7

(8) 1 × 3 = 3   (18) 1 × 2 = 2

(9) 1 × 9 = 9   (19) 1 × 8 = 8

(10) 1 × 5 = 5   (20) 1 × 6 = 6

Practicing Numbers

2 – 20

Name

Date

To parents
Multiplying by 2 is much more difficult than multiplying by 1. Please help your child use this page to practice skip-counting by 2s, which is a good way to prepare for multiplying with the number.

■ Say each number aloud as you trace it.

1	2	3	4	5	6	7	8	9	10
11	12	13	14	15	16	17	18	19	20
21	22	23	24	25	26	27	28	29	30
31	32	33	34	35	36	37	38	39	40
41	42	43	44	45	46	47	48	49	50

2	4	6	8	10	12	14	16	18	20

(1) $2 + 2 = 4$

(2) $2 + 2 + 2 = 6$

(3) $2 + 2 + 2 + 2 = 8$

(4) $2 + 2 + 2 + 2 + 2 = 10$

(5) $2 + 2 + 2 + 2 + 2 + 2 = 12$

(6) $2 + 2 + 2 + 2 + 2 + 2 + 2 = 14$

(7) $2 + 2 + 2 + 2 + 2 + 2 + 2 + 2 = 16$

(8) $2 + 2 + 2 + 2 + 2 + 2 + 2 + 2 + 2 = 18$

(9) $2 + 2 + 2 + 2 + 2 + 2 + 2 + 2 + 2 + 2 = 20$

■ Draw a line from 2 to 20 in order while saying each number aloud.

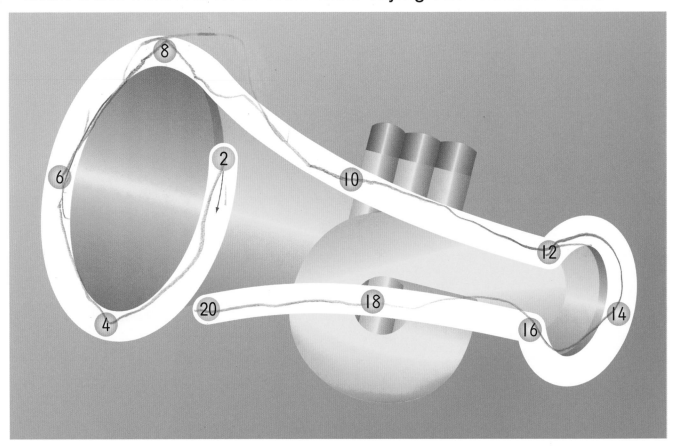

■ Add the numbers below.

(1) 2 + 2 = 4

(2) 2 + 2 + 2 = 6

(3) 2 + 2 + 2 + 2 = 8

(4) 2 + 2 + 2 + 2 + 2 = 10

(5) 2 + 2 + 2 + 2 + 2 + 2 = 12

(6) 2 + 2 + 2 + 2 + 2 + 2 + 2 = 14

(7) 2 + 2 + 2 + 2 + 2 + 2 + 2 + 2 = 16

(8) 2 + 2 + 2 + 2 + 2 + 2 + 2 + 2 + 2 = 18

(9) 2 + 2 + 2 + 2 + 2 + 2 + 2 + 2 + 2 + 2 = 20

Practicing Repeated Addition

2 to 10

Name

Date

■ Say each number aloud as you trace it.

2	4	6	8	10

(1) $2 + 2 = 4$

(2) $2 + 2 + 2 = 6$

(3) $2 + 2 + 2 + 2 = 8$

(4) $2 + 2 + 2 + 2 + 2 = 10$

■ Write the numbers in the number line. Then add the numbers below.

2	4	6	8	10

(1) $2 + 2 = 4$

(2) $2 + 2 + 2 = 6$

(3) $2 + 2 + 2 + 2 = 8$

(4) $2 + 2 + 2 + 2 + 2 = 10$

12 to 20

■ Say each number aloud as you trace it.

| 12 | 14 | 16 | 18 | 20 |

(1) $2+2+2+2+2+2=$ 12

(2) $2+2+2+2+2+2+2=$ 14

(3) $2+2+2+2+2+2+2+2=$ 16

(4) $2+2+2+2+2+2+2+2+2=$ 18

(5) $2+2+2+2+2+2+2+2+2+2=$ 20

■ Write the numbers in the number line. Then add the numbers below.

| 12 | 14 | 16 | 18 | 20 |

(1) $2+2+2+2+2+2=$ 12

(2) $2+2+2+2+2+2+2=$ 14

(3) $2+2+2+2+2+2+2+2=$ 16

(4) $2+2+2+2+2+2+2+2+2=$ 18

(5) $2+2+2+2+2+2+2+2+2+2=$ 20

Name

Date

■ Read the multiplication table aloud.

Multiplication Table

(1)	2	×	1	=	2

Two times one is two.

(2) 2 × 2 = 4   Two times two is four.

(3) 2 × 3 = 6   Two times three is six.

(4) 2 × 4 = 8   Two times four is eight.

(5) 2 × 5 = 10   Two times five is ten.

(6) 2 × 6 = 12   Two times six is twelve.

(7) 2 × 7 = 14   Two times seven is fourteen.

(8) 2 × 8 = 16   Two times eight is sixteen.

(9) 2 × 9 = 18   Two times nine is eighteen.

(10) 2 × 10 = 20 Two times ten is twenty.

■ Read each number sentence aloud as you trace the answer.

(1) 2 × 1 = 2

(2) 2 × 2 = 4

(3) 2 × 3 = 6

(4) 2 × 4 = 8

(5) 2 × 5 = 10

(6) 2 × 6 = 12

(7) 2 × 7 = 14

(8) 2 × 8 = 16

(9) 2 × 9 = 18

(10) 2 × 10 = 20

2×1 to 2×10

■ Multiply the numbers below.

(1) 2 × 1 = 2

(2) 2 × 2 = 4

(3) 2 × 3 = 6

(4) 2 × 4 = 8

(5) 2 × 5 = 10

(6) 2 × 6 = 12

(7) 2 × 7 = 14

(8) 2 × 8 = 16

(9) 2 × 9 = 18

(10) 2 × 10 = 20

(11) 2 × 1 = 2

(12) 2 × 2 = 4

(13) 2 × 3 = 6

(14) 2 × 4 = 8

(15) 2 × 5 = 10

(16) 2 × 6 = 12

(17) 2 × 7 = 14

(18) 2 × 8 = 16

(19) 2 × 9 = 18

(20) 2 × 10 = 20

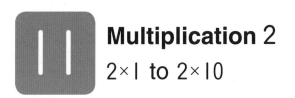

Multiplication 2
2×1 to 2×10

■ Multiply the numbers below.

(1) 2 × 3 = 6

(2) 2 × 6 = 12

(3) 2 × 9 = 18

(4) 2 × 5 = 10

(5) 2 × 1 = 2

(6) 2 × 7 = 14

(7) 2 × 2 = 4

(8) 2 × 8 = 16

(9) 2 × 10 = 20

(10) 2 × 4 = 8

(11) 2 × 9 = 18

(12) 2 × 1 = 2

(13) 2 × 7 = 14

(14) 2 × 10 = 20

(15) 2 × 8 = 16

(16) 2 × 3 = 6

(17) 2 × 5 = 10

(18) 2 × 2 = 4

(19) 2 × 4 = 8

(20) 2 × 6 = 12

2×1 to 2×10

■ Multiply the numbers below.

(1) 2 × 4 = 8

(11) 2 × 9 = 18

(2) 2 × 7 = 14

(12) 2 × 3 = 6

(3) 2 × 10 = 20

(13) 2 × 1 = 2

(4) 2 × 2 = 4

(14) 2 × 4 = 8

(5) 2 × 6 = 12

(15) 2 × 10 = 20

(6) 2 × 1 = 2

(16) 2 × 5 = 18

(7) 2 × 8 = 16

(17) 2 × 7 = 14

(8) 2 × 3 = 6

(18) 2 × 2 = 4

(9) 2 × 9 = 18

(19) 2 × 8 = 16

(10) 2 × 5 = 10

(20) 2 × 6 = 12

Name

Date

■ Multiply the numbers below.

(1) $2 \times 7 = 14$

(2) $2 \times 3 = 6$

(3) $2 \times 6 = 12$

(4) $2 \times 1 = 2$

(5) $2 \times 10 = 20$

(6) $2 \times 5 = 10$

(7) $2 \times 9 = 18$

(8) $2 \times 4 = 8$

(9) $2 \times 2 = 4$

(10) $2 \times 8 = 16$

(11) $2 \times 2 = 4$

(12) $2 \times 5 = 10$

(13) $2 \times 9 = 18$

(14) $2 \times 7 = 14$

(15) $2 \times 3 = 6$

(16) $2 \times 1 = 2$

(17) $2 \times 8 = 16$

(18) $2 \times 6 = 12$

(19) $2 \times 4 = 8$

(20) $2 \times 10 = 20$

2×1 to 2×10

■ Multiply the numbers below.

(1) 2 × 1 = 2

(2) 2 × 8 = 16

(3) 2 × 10 = 20

(4) 2 × 3 = 6

(5) 2 × 6 = 12

(6) 2 × 2 = 4

(7) 2 × 7 = 14

(8) 2 × 4 = 8

(9) 2 × 5 = 10

(10) 2 × 9 = 18

(11) 2 × 4 = 8

(12) 2 × 9 = 18

(13) 2 × 1 = 2

(14) 2 × 5 = 10

(15) 2 × 10 = 20

(16) 2 × 6 = 12

(17) 2 × 2 = 4

(18) 2 × 8 = 16

(19) 2 × 3 = 6

(20) 2 × 7 = 14

Name

Date

■ Multiply the numbers below.

(1) $1 \times 1 = 1$

(2) $1 \times 2 = 2$

(3) $1 \times 3 = 3$

(4) $1 \times 4 = 4$

(5) $1 \times 5 = 5$

(6) $1 \times 6 = 6$

(7) $1 \times 7 = 7$

(8) $1 \times 8 = 8$

(9) $1 \times 9 = 9$

(10) $1 \times 10 = 10$

(11) $2 \times 1 = 2$

(12) $2 \times 2 = 4$

(13) $2 \times 3 = 6$

(14) $2 \times 4 = 8$

(15) $2 \times 5 = 10$

(16) $2 \times 6 = 12$

(17) $2 \times 7 = 14$

(18) $2 \times 8 = 16$

(19) $2 \times 9 = 18$

(20) $2 \times 10 = 20$

Multiplication 1, 2

■ Multiply the numbers below.

(1) $1 \times 4 =$

(2) $1 \times 7 =$

(3) $1 \times 10 =$

(4) $1 \times 2 =$

(5) $1 \times 6 =$

(6) $1 \times 1 =$

(7) $1 \times 8 =$

(8) $1 \times 3 =$

(9) $1 \times 9 =$

(10) $1 \times 5 =$

(11) $2 \times 4 =$

(12) $2 \times 9 =$

(13) $2 \times 1 =$

(14) $2 \times 5 =$

(15) $2 \times 10 =$

(16) $2 \times 6 =$

(17) $2 \times 2 =$

(18) $2 \times 8 =$

(19) $2 \times 3 =$

(20) $2 \times 7 =$

Review
Multiplication 1, 2

■ Multiply the numbers below.

(1) $1 \times 3 =$

(2) $2 \times 7 =$

(3) $1 \times 9 =$

(4) $2 \times 4 =$

(5) $1 \times 6 =$

(6) $2 \times 10 =$

(7) $1 \times 1 =$

(8) $2 \times 8 =$

(9) $1 \times 2 =$

(10) $2 \times 5 =$

(11) $2 \times 2 =$

(12) $1 \times 8 =$

(13) $2 \times 6 =$

(14) $1 \times 10 =$

(15) $2 \times 9 =$

(16) $1 \times 5 =$

(17) $2 \times 3 =$

(18) $1 \times 7 =$

(19) $2 \times 1 =$

(20) $1 \times 4 =$

Multiplication 1, 2

■ Multiply the numbers below.

(1) $2 \times 9 =$

(2) $1 \times 7 =$

(3) $2 \times 5 =$

(4) $1 \times 6 =$

(5) $2 \times 1 =$

(6) $1 \times 8 =$

(7) $2 \times 10 =$

(8) $1 \times 3 =$

(9) $2 \times 2 =$

(10) $1 \times 4 =$

(11) $1 \times 10 =$

(12) $2 \times 3 =$

(13) $1 \times 1 =$

(14) $2 \times 8 =$

(15) $1 \times 5 =$

(16) $2 \times 6 =$

(17) $1 \times 2 =$

(18) $2 \times 4 =$

(19) $1 \times 9 =$

(20) $2 \times 7 =$

Name

Date

■ Say each number aloud as you trace it.

1	2	3	4	5	6	7	8	9	10
11	12	13	14	15	16	17	18	19	20
21	22	23	24	25	26	27	28	29	30
31	32	33	34	35	36	37	38	39	40
41	42	43	44	45	46	47	48	49	50

3	6	9	12	15	18	21	24	27	30

(1) $3 + 3 = 6$

(2) $3 + 3 + 3 = 9$

(3) $3 + 3 + 3 + 3 = 12$

(4) $3 + 3 + 3 + 3 + 3 = 15$

(5) $3 + 3 + 3 + 3 + 3 + 3 = 18$

(6) $3 + 3 + 3 + 3 + 3 + 3 + 3 = 21$

(7) $3 + 3 + 3 + 3 + 3 + 3 + 3 + 3 = 24$

(8) $3 + 3 + 3 + 3 + 3 + 3 + 3 + 3 + 3 = 27$

(9) $3 + 3 + 3 + 3 + 3 + 3 + 3 + 3 + 3 + 3 = 30$

■ Draw a line from 3 to 30 in order while saying each number aloud.

■ Add the numbers below.

(1) 3 + 3 =

(2) 3 + 3 + 3 =

(3) 3 + 3 + 3 + 3 =

(4) 3 + 3 + 3 + 3 + 3 =

(5) 3 + 3 + 3 + 3 + 3 + 3 =

(6) 3 + 3 + 3 + 3 + 3 + 3 + 3 =

(7) 3 + 3 + 3 + 3 + 3 + 3 + 3 + 3 =

(8) 3 + 3 + 3 + 3 + 3 + 3 + 3 + 3 + 3 =

(9) 3 + 3 + 3 + 3 + 3 + 3 + 3 + 3 + 3 + 3 =

Practicing Repeated Addition

3 to 15

Name

Date

■ Say each number aloud as you trace it.

3	6	9	12	15

(1) $3 + 3 = 6$

(2) $3 + 3 + 3 = 9$

(3) $3 + 3 + 3 + 3 = 12$

(4) $3 + 3 + 3 + 3 + 3 = 15$

■ Write the numbers in the number line. Then add the numbers below.

3				

(1) $3 + 3 =$

(2) $3 + 3 + 3 =$

(3) $3 + 3 + 3 + 3 =$

(4) $3 + 3 + 3 + 3 + 3 =$

18 to 30

■ Say each number aloud as you trace it.

18	21	24	27	30

(1) $3+3+3+3+3+3 = 18$

(2) $3+3+3+3+3+3+3 = 21$

(3) $3+3+3+3+3+3+3+3 = 24$

(4) $3+3+3+3+3+3+3+3+3 = 27$

(5) $3+3+3+3+3+3+3+3+3+3 = 30$

■ Write the numbers in the number line. Then add the numbers below.

18				

(1) $3+3+3+3+3+3 =$

(2) $3+3+3+3+3+3+3 =$

(3) $3+3+3+3+3+3+3+3 =$

(4) $3+3+3+3+3+3+3+3+3 =$

(5) $3+3+3+3+3+3+3+3+3+3 =$

17 Multiplication 3

3×1 to 3×10

Name
Date

■ Read the multiplication table aloud.

Multiplication Table

(1)	3	×	1	=	3	Three times one is three.
(2)	3	×	2	=	6	Three times two is six.
(3)	3	×	3	=	9	Three times three is nine.
(4)	3	×	4	=	12	Three times four is twelve.
(5)	3	×	5	=	15	Three times five is fifteen.
(6)	3	×	6	=	18	Three times six is eighteen.
(7)	3	×	7	=	21	Three times seven is twenty-one.
(8)	3	×	8	=	24	Three times eight is twenty-four.
(9)	3	×	9	=	27	Three times nine is twenty-seven.
(10)	3	×	10	=	30	Three times ten is thirty.

■ Read each number sentence aloud as you trace the answer.

(1) 3 × 1 = 3   (6) 3 × 6 = 18

(2) 3 × 2 = 6   (7) 3 × 7 = 21

(3) 3 × 3 = 9   (8) 3 × 8 = 24

(4) 3 × 4 = 12   (9) 3 × 9 = 27

(5) 3 × 5 = 15   (10) 3 × 10 = 30

■ Multiply the numbers below.

(1) 3 × 1 =

(2) 3 × 2 =

(3) 3 × 3 =

(4) 3 × 4 =

(5) 3 × 5 =

(6) 3 × 6 =

(7) 3 × 7 =

(8) 3 × 8 =

(9) 3 × 9 =

(10) 3 × 10 =

(11) 3 × 1 =

(12) 3 × 2 =

(13) 3 × 3 =

(14) 3 × 4 =

(15) 3 × 5 =

(16) 3 × 6 =

(17) 3 × 7 =

(18) 3 × 8 =

(19) 3 × 9 =

(20) 3 × 10 =

Name

Date

■ Multiply the numbers below.

(1) 3 × 3 =   (11) 3 × 9 =

(2) 3 × 6 =   (12) 3 × 1 =

(3) 3 × 9 =   (13) 3 × 7 =

(4) 3 × 5 =   (14) 3 × 10 =

(5) 3 × 1 =   (15) 3 × 8 =

(6) 3 × 7 =   (16) 3 × 3 =

(7) 3 × 2 =   (17) 3 × 5 =

(8) 3 × 8 =   (18) 3 × 2 =

(9) 3 × 10 =   (19) 3 × 4 =

(10) 3 × 4 =   (20) 3 × 6 =

3×1 to 3×10

■ Multiply the numbers below.

(1) 3 × 4 =

(2) 3 × 7 =

(3) 3 × 10 =

(4) 3 × 2 =

(5) 3 × 6 =

(6) 3 × 1 =

(7) 3 × 8 =

(8) 3 × 3 =

(9) 3 × 9 =

(10) 3 × 5 =

(11) 3 × 9 =

(12) 3 × 3 =

(13) 3 × 1 =

(14) 3 × 4 =

(15) 3 × 10 =

(16) 3 × 5 =

(17) 3 × 7 =

(18) 3 × 2 =

(19) 3 × 8 =

(20) 3 × 6 =

Name	
Date	

■ Multiply the numbers below.

(1) 3 × 7 =

(2) 3 × 3 =

(3) 3 × 6 =

(4) 3 × 1 =

(5) 3 × 10 =

(6) 3 × 5 =

(7) 3 × 9 =

(8) 3 × 4 =

(9) 3 × 2 =

(10) 3 × 8 =

(11) 3 × 2 =

(12) 3 × 5 =

(13) 3 × 9 =

(14) 3 × 7 =

(15) 3 × 3 =

(16) 3 × 1 =

(17) 3 × 8 =

(18) 3 × 6 =

(19) 3 × 4 =

(20) 3 × 10 =

■ Multiply the numbers below.

(1) $3 \times 1 =$

(2) $3 \times 8 =$

(3) $3 \times 10 =$

(4) $3 \times 3 =$

(5) $3 \times 6 =$

(6) $3 \times 2 =$

(7) $3 \times 7 =$

(8) $3 \times 4 =$

(9) $3 \times 5 =$

(10) $3 \times 9 =$

(11) $3 \times 4 =$

(12) $3 \times 9 =$

(13) $3 \times 1 =$

(14) $3 \times 5 =$

(15) $3 \times 10 =$

(16) $3 \times 6 =$

(17) $3 \times 2 =$

(18) $3 \times 8 =$

(19) $3 \times 3 =$

(20) $3 \times 7 =$

Name

Date

■ Multiply the numbers below.

(1) $2 \times 1 =$ (11) $3 \times 1 =$

(2) $2 \times 2 =$ (12) $3 \times 2 =$

(3) $2 \times 3 =$ (13) $3 \times 3 =$

(4) $2 \times 4 =$ (14) $3 \times 4 =$

(5) $2 \times 5 =$ (15) $3 \times 5 =$

(6) $2 \times 6 =$ (16) $3 \times 6 =$

(7) $2 \times 7 =$ (17) $3 \times 7 =$

(8) $2 \times 8 =$ (18) $3 \times 8 =$

(9) $2 \times 9 =$ (19) $3 \times 9 =$

(10) $2 \times 10 =$ (20) $3 \times 10 =$

Multiplication 2, 3

■ Multiply the numbers below.

(1) $2 \times 4 =$ (11) $3 \times 4 =$

(2) $2 \times 7 =$ (12) $3 \times 9 =$

(3) $2 \times 10 =$ (13) $3 \times 1 =$

(4) $2 \times 2 =$ (14) $3 \times 5 =$

(5) $2 \times 6 =$ (15) $3 \times 10 =$

(6) $2 \times 1 =$ (16) $3 \times 6 =$

(7) $2 \times 8 =$ (17) $3 \times 2 =$

(8) $2 \times 3 =$ (18) $3 \times 8 =$

(9) $2 \times 9 =$ (19) $3 \times 3 =$

(10) $2 \times 5 =$ (20) $3 \times 7 =$

Name

Date

■ Multiply the numbers below.

(1) $2 \times 3 =$

(2) $3 \times 7 =$

(3) $2 \times 9 =$

(4) $3 \times 4 =$

(5) $2 \times 6 =$

(6) $3 \times 10 =$

(7) $2 \times 1 =$

(8) $3 \times 8 =$

(9) $2 \times 2 =$

(10) $3 \times 5 =$

(11) $3 \times 2 =$

(12) $2 \times 8 =$

(13) $3 \times 6 =$

(14) $2 \times 10 =$

(15) $3 \times 9 =$

(16) $2 \times 5 =$

(17) $3 \times 3 =$

(18) $2 \times 7 =$

(19) $3 \times 1 =$

(20) $2 \times 4 =$

Multiplication 2, 3

■ Multiply the numbers below.

(1) $3 \times 9 =$

(2) $2 \times 7 =$

(3) $3 \times 5 =$

(4) $2 \times 6 =$

(5) $3 \times 1 =$

(6) $2 \times 8 =$

(7) $3 \times 10 =$

(8) $2 \times 3 =$

(9) $3 \times 2 =$

(10) $2 \times 4 =$

(11) $2 \times 10 =$

(12) $3 \times 3 =$

(13) $2 \times 1 =$

(14) $3 \times 8 =$

(15) $2 \times 5 =$

(16) $3 \times 6 =$

(17) $2 \times 2 =$

(18) $3 \times 4 =$

(19) $2 \times 9 =$

(20) $3 \times 7 =$

Name

Date

■ Say each number aloud as you trace it.

1	2	3	4	5	6	7	8	9	10
11	12	13	14	15	16	17	18	19	20
21	22	23	24	25	26	27	28	29	30
31	32	33	34	35	36	37	38	39	40
41	42	43	44	45	46	47	48	49	50

4	8	12	16	20	24	28	32	36	40

(1) $4 + 4 = 8$

(2) $4 + 4 + 4 = 12$

(3) $4 + 4 + 4 + 4 = 16$

(4) $4 + 4 + 4 + 4 + 4 = 20$

(5) $4 + 4 + 4 + 4 + 4 + 4 = 24$

(6) $4 + 4 + 4 + 4 + 4 + 4 + 4 = 28$

(7) $4 + 4 + 4 + 4 + 4 + 4 + 4 + 4 = 32$

(8) $4 + 4 + 4 + 4 + 4 + 4 + 4 + 4 + 4 = 36$

(9) $4 + 4 + 4 + 4 + 4 + 4 + 4 + 4 + 4 + 4 = 40$

■ Draw a line from 4 to 40 in order while saying each number aloud.

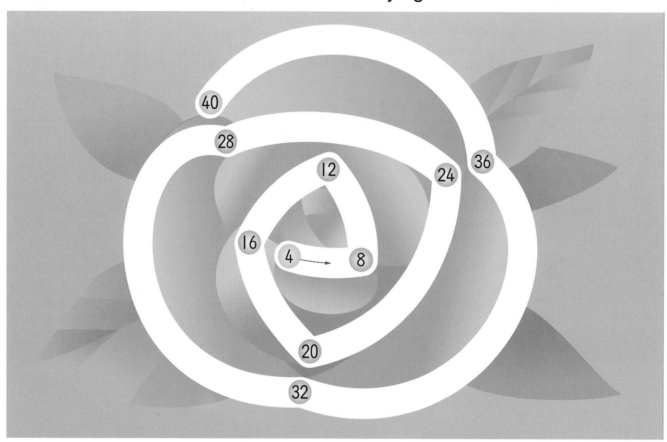

■ Add the numbers below.

(1) 4 + 4 =

(2) 4 + 4 + 4 =

(3) 4 + 4 + 4 + 4 =

(4) 4 + 4 + 4 + 4 + 4 =

(5) 4 + 4 + 4 + 4 + 4 + 4 =

(6) 4 + 4 + 4 + 4 + 4 + 4 + 4 =

(7) 4 + 4 + 4 + 4 + 4 + 4 + 4 + 4 =

(8) 4 + 4 + 4 + 4 + 4 + 4 + 4 + 4 + 4 =

(9) 4 + 4 + 4 + 4 + 4 + 4 + 4 + 4 + 4 + 4 =

23 **Practicing Repeated Addition**

4 to 20

Name

Date

■ Say each number aloud as you trace it.

4	8	12	16	20

(1) $4 + 4 = 8$

(2) $4 + 4 + 4 = 12$

(3) $4 + 4 + 4 + 4 = 16$

(4) $4 + 4 + 4 + 4 + 4 = 20$

■ Write the numbers in the number line. Then add the numbers below.

4				

(1) $4 + 4 =$

(2) $4 + 4 + 4 =$

(3) $4 + 4 + 4 + 4 =$

(4) $4 + 4 + 4 + 4 + 4 =$

24 to 40

■ Say each number aloud as you trace it.

| 24 | 28 | 32 | 36 | 40 |

(1) $4 + 4 + 4 + 4 + 4 + 4 = 24$

(2) $4 + 4 + 4 + 4 + 4 + 4 + 4 = 28$

(3) $4 + 4 + 4 + 4 + 4 + 4 + 4 + 4 = 32$

(4) $4 + 4 + 4 + 4 + 4 + 4 + 4 + 4 + 4 = 36$

(5) $4 + 4 + 4 + 4 + 4 + 4 + 4 + 4 + 4 + 4 = 40$

■ Write the numbers in the number line. Then add the numbers below.

| 24 | | | | |

(1) $4 + 4 + 4 + 4 + 4 + 4 =$

(2) $4 + 4 + 4 + 4 + 4 + 4 + 4 =$

(3) $4 + 4 + 4 + 4 + 4 + 4 + 4 + 4 =$

(4) $4 + 4 + 4 + 4 + 4 + 4 + 4 + 4 + 4 =$

(5) $4 + 4 + 4 + 4 + 4 + 4 + 4 + 4 + 4 + 4 =$

Multiplication 4

4×1 to 4×10

Name

Date

■ Read the multiplication table aloud.

Multiplication Table

(1) 4 × 1 = 4   Four times one is four.

(2) 4 × 2 = 8   Four times two is eight.

(3) 4 × 3 = 12   Four times three is twelve.

(4) 4 × 4 = 16   Four times four is sixteen.

(5) 4 × 5 = 20   Four times five is twenty.

(6) 4 × 6 = 24   Four times six is twenty-four.

(7) 4 × 7 = 28   Four times seven is twenty-eight.

(8) 4 × 8 = 32   Four times eight is thirty-two.

(9) 4 × 9 = 36   Four times nine is thirty-six.

(10) 4 × 10 = 40   Four times ten is forty.

■ Read each number sentence aloud as you trace the answer.

(1) 4 × 1 = 4   (6) 4 × 6 = 24

(2) 4 × 2 = 8   (7) 4 × 7 = 28

(3) 4 × 3 = 12   (8) 4 × 8 = 32

(4) 4 × 4 = 16   (9) 4 × 9 = 36

(5) 4 × 5 = 20   (10) 4 × 10 = 40

4×1 to 4×10

■ Multiply the numbers below.

(1) 4 × 1 =   (11) 4 × 1 =

(2) 4 × 2 =   (12) 4 × 2 =

(3) 4 × 3 =   (13) 4 × 3 =

(4) 4 × 4 =   (14) 4 × 4 =

(5) 4 × 5 =   (15) 4 × 5 =

(6) 4 × 6 =   (16) 4 × 6 =

(7) 4 × 7 =   (17) 4 × 7 =

(8) 4 × 8 =   (18) 4 × 8 =

(9) 4 × 9 =   (19) 4 × 9 =

(10) 4 × 10 =   (20) 4 × 10 =

Name

Date

■ Multiply the numbers below.

(1) $4 \times 3 =$

(2) $4 \times 6 =$

(3) $4 \times 9 =$

(4) $4 \times 5 =$

(5) $4 \times 1 =$

(6) $4 \times 7 =$

(7) $4 \times 2 =$

(8) $4 \times 8 =$

(9) $4 \times 10 =$

(10) $4 \times 4 =$

(11) $4 \times 9 =$

(12) $4 \times 1 =$

(13) $4 \times 7 =$

(14) $4 \times 10 =$

(15) $4 \times 8 =$

(16) $4 \times 3 =$

(17) $4 \times 5 =$

(18) $4 \times 2 =$

(19) $4 \times 4 =$

(20) $4 \times 6 =$

4×1 to 4×10

■ Multiply the numbers below.

(1) 4 × 4 =

(2) 4 × 7 =

(3) 4 × 10 =

(4) 4 × 2 =

(5) 4 × 6 =

(6) 4 × 1 =

(7) 4 × 8 =

(8) 4 × 3 =

(9) 4 × 9 =

(10) 4 × 5 =

(11) 4 × 9 =

(12) 4 × 3 =

(13) 4 × 1 =

(14) 4 × 4 =

(15) 4 × 10 =

(16) 4 × 5 =

(17) 4 × 7 =

(18) 4 × 2 =

(19) 4 × 8 =

(20) 4 × 6 =

Multiplication 4
4×1 to 4×10

Name

Date

■ Multiply the numbers below.

(1) $4 \times 7 =$

(2) $4 \times 3 =$

(3) $4 \times 6 =$

(4) $4 \times 1 =$

(5) $4 \times 10 =$

(6) $4 \times 5 =$

(7) $4 \times 9 =$

(8) $4 \times 4 =$

(9) $4 \times 2 =$

(10) $4 \times 8 =$

(11) $4 \times 2 =$

(12) $4 \times 5 =$

(13) $4 \times 9 =$

(14) $4 \times 7 =$

(15) $4 \times 3 =$

(16) $4 \times 1 =$

(17) $4 \times 8 =$

(18) $4 \times 6 =$

(19) $4 \times 4 =$

(20) $4 \times 10 =$

4×1 to 4×10

■ Multiply the numbers below.

(1) 4 × 1 =

(2) 4 × 8 =

(3) 4 × 10 =

(4) 4 × 3 =

(5) 4 × 6 =

(6) 4 × 2 =

(7) 4 × 7 =

(8) 4 × 4 =

(9) 4 × 5 =

(10) 4 × 9 =

(11) 4 × 4 =

(12) 4 × 9 =

(13) 4 × 1 =

(14) 4 × 5 =

(15) 4 × 10 =

(16) 4 × 6 =

(17) 4 × 2 =

(18) 4 × 8 =

(19) 4 × 3 =

(20) 4 × 7 =

Name

Date

■ Multiply the numbers below.

(1) $3 \times 1 =$

(2) $3 \times 2 =$

(3) $3 \times 3 =$

(4) $3 \times 4 =$

(5) $3 \times 5 =$

(6) $3 \times 6 =$

(7) $3 \times 7 =$

(8) $3 \times 8 =$

(9) $3 \times 9 =$

(10) $3 \times 10 =$

(11) $4 \times 1 =$

(12) $4 \times 2 =$

(13) $4 \times 3 =$

(14) $4 \times 4 =$

(15) $4 \times 5 =$

(16) $4 \times 6 =$

(17) $4 \times 7 =$

(18) $4 \times 8 =$

(19) $4 \times 9 =$

(20) $4 \times 10 =$

Multiplication 3, 4

■ Multiply the numbers below.

(1) $3 \times 4 =$

(2) $3 \times 7 =$

(3) $3 \times 10 =$

(4) $3 \times 2 =$

(5) $3 \times 6 =$

(6) $3 \times 1 =$

(7) $3 \times 8 =$

(8) $3 \times 3 =$

(9) $3 \times 9 =$

(10) $3 \times 5 =$

(11) $4 \times 4 =$

(12) $4 \times 9 =$

(13) $4 \times 1 =$

(14) $4 \times 5 =$

(15) $4 \times 10 =$

(16) $4 \times 6 =$

(17) $4 \times 2 =$

(18) $4 \times 8 =$

(19) $4 \times 3 =$

(20) $4 \times 7 =$

28 Review
Multiplication 3, 4

Name

Date

■ Multiply the numbers below.

(1) $3 \times 3 =$

(2) $4 \times 7 =$

(3) $3 \times 9 =$

(4) $4 \times 4 =$

(5) $3 \times 6 =$

(6) $4 \times 10 =$

(7) $3 \times 1 =$

(8) $4 \times 8 =$

(9) $3 \times 2 =$

(10) $4 \times 5 =$

(11) $4 \times 2 =$

(12) $3 \times 8 =$

(13) $4 \times 6 =$

(14) $3 \times 10 =$

(15) $4 \times 9 =$

(16) $3 \times 5 =$

(17) $4 \times 3 =$

(18) $3 \times 7 =$

(19) $4 \times 1 =$

(20) $3 \times 4 =$

Multiplication 3, 4

■ Multiply the numbers below.

(1) $3 \times 9 =$

(2) $4 \times 7 =$

(3) $3 \times 5 =$

(4) $4 \times 6 =$

(5) $3 \times 1 =$

(6) $4 \times 8 =$

(7) $3 \times 10 =$

(8) $4 \times 3 =$

(9) $3 \times 2 =$

(10) $4 \times 4 =$

(11) $3 \times 10 =$

(12) $4 \times 3 =$

(13) $3 \times 1 =$

(14) $4 \times 8 =$

(15) $3 \times 5 =$

(16) $4 \times 6 =$

(17) $3 \times 2 =$

(18) $4 \times 4 =$

(19) $3 \times 9 =$

(20) $4 \times 7 =$

Practicing Numbers

5 – 50

Name

Date

■ Say each number aloud as you trace it.

1	2	3	4	5	6	7	8	9	10
11	12	13	14	15	16	17	18	19	20
21	22	23	24	25	26	27	28	29	30
31	32	33	34	35	36	37	38	39	40
41	42	43	44	45	46	47	48	49	50

5	10	15	20	25	30	35	40	45	50

(1) $5 + 5 = 10$

(2) $5 + 5 + 5 = 15$

(3) $5 + 5 + 5 + 5 = 20$

(4) $5 + 5 + 5 + 5 + 5 = 25$

(5) $5 + 5 + 5 + 5 + 5 + 5 = 30$

(6) $5 + 5 + 5 + 5 + 5 + 5 + 5 = 35$

(7) $5 + 5 + 5 + 5 + 5 + 5 + 5 + 5 = 40$

(8) $5 + 5 + 5 + 5 + 5 + 5 + 5 + 5 + 5 = 45$

(9) $5 + 5 + 5 + 5 + 5 + 5 + 5 + 5 + 5 + 5 = 50$

■ Draw a line from 5 to 50 in order while saying each number aloud.

■ Add the numbers below.

(1) $5 + 5 =$

(2) $5 + 5 + 5 =$

(3) $5 + 5 + 5 + 5 =$

(4) $5 + 5 + 5 + 5 + 5 =$

(5) $5 + 5 + 5 + 5 + 5 + 5 =$

(6) $5 + 5 + 5 + 5 + 5 + 5 + 5 =$

(7) $5 + 5 + 5 + 5 + 5 + 5 + 5 + 5 =$

(8) $5 + 5 + 5 + 5 + 5 + 5 + 5 + 5 + 5 =$

(9) $5 + 5 + 5 + 5 + 5 + 5 + 5 + 5 + 5 + 5 =$

Practicing Repeated Addition

5 to 25

Name

Date

■ Say each number aloud as you trace it.

| 5 | 10 | 15 | 20 | 25 |

(1) 5 + 5 = 10

(2) 5 + 5 + 5 = 15

(3) 5 + 5 + 5 + 5 = 20

(4) 5 + 5 + 5 + 5 + 5 = 25

■ Write the numbers in the number line. Then add the numbers below.

| 5 | | | | |

(1) 5 + 5 =

(2) 5 + 5 + 5 =

(3) 5 + 5 + 5 + 5 =

(4) 5 + 5 + 5 + 5 + 5 =

30 to 50

■ Say each number aloud as you trace it.

30	35	40	45	50

(1) $5 + 5 + 5 + 5 + 5 + 5 = 30$

(2) $5 + 5 + 5 + 5 + 5 + 5 + 5 = 35$

(3) $5 + 5 + 5 + 5 + 5 + 5 + 5 + 5 = 40$

(4) $5 + 5 + 5 + 5 + 5 + 5 + 5 + 5 + 5 = 45$

(5) $5 + 5 + 5 + 5 + 5 + 5 + 5 + 5 + 5 + 5 = 50$

■ Write the numbers in the number line. Then add the numbers below.

30				

(1) $5 + 5 + 5 + 5 + 5 + 5 =$

(2) $5 + 5 + 5 + 5 + 5 + 5 + 5 =$

(3) $5 + 5 + 5 + 5 + 5 + 5 + 5 + 5 =$

(4) $5 + 5 + 5 + 5 + 5 + 5 + 5 + 5 + 5 =$

(5) $5 + 5 + 5 + 5 + 5 + 5 + 5 + 5 + 5 + 5 =$

31

Multiplication 5
5×1 to 5×10

Name

Date

■ Read the multiplication table aloud.

Multiplication Table

(1)	$5 \times 1 = 5$	Five times one is five.
(2)	$5 \times 2 = 10$	Five times two is ten.
(3)	$5 \times 3 = 15$	Five times three is fifteen.
(4)	$5 \times 4 = 20$	Five times four is twenty.
(5)	$5 \times 5 = 25$	Five times five is twenty-five.
(6)	$5 \times 6 = 30$	Five times six is thirty.
(7)	$5 \times 7 = 35$	Five times seven is thirty-five.
(8)	$5 \times 8 = 40$	Five times eight is forty.
(9)	$5 \times 9 = 45$	Five times nine is forty-five.
(10)	$5 \times 10 = 50$	Five times ten is fifty.

■ Read each number sentence aloud as you trace the answer.

(1) $5 \times 1 = 5$

(2) $5 \times 2 = 10$

(3) $5 \times 3 = 15$

(4) $5 \times 4 = 20$

(5) $5 \times 5 = 25$

(6) $5 \times 6 = 30$

(7) $5 \times 7 = 35$

(8) $5 \times 8 = 40$

(9) $5 \times 9 = 45$

(10) $5 \times 10 = 50$

5×1 to 5×10

■ Multiply the numbers below.

(1) 5 × 1 =

(2) 5 × 2 =

(3) 5 × 3 =

(4) 5 × 4 =

(5) 5 × 5 =

(6) 5 × 6 =

(7) 5 × 7 =

(8) 5 × 8 =

(9) 5 × 9 =

(10) 5 × 10 =

(11) 5 × 1 =

(12) 5 × 2 =

(13) 5 × 3 =

(14) 5 × 4 =

(15) 5 × 5 =

(16) 5 × 6 =

(17) 5 × 7 =

(18) 5 × 8 =

(19) 5 × 9 =

(20) 5 × 10 =

32

Name

Date

■ Multiply the numbers below.

(1) $5 \times 3 =$

(2) $5 \times 6 =$

(3) $5 \times 9 =$

(4) $5 \times 5 =$

(5) $5 \times 1 =$

(6) $5 \times 7 =$

(7) $5 \times 2 =$

(8) $5 \times 8 =$

(9) $5 \times 10 =$

(10) $5 \times 4 =$

(11) $5 \times 9 =$

(12) $5 \times 1 =$

(13) $5 \times 7 =$

(14) $5 \times 10 =$

(15) $5 \times 8 =$

(16) $5 \times 3 =$

(17) $5 \times 5 =$

(18) $5 \times 2 =$

(19) $5 \times 4 =$

(20) $5 \times 6 =$

■ Multiply the numbers below.

(1) $5 \times 4 =$

(2) $5 \times 7 =$

(3) $5 \times 10 =$

(4) $5 \times 2 =$

(5) $5 \times 6 =$

(6) $5 \times 1 =$

(7) $5 \times 8 =$

(8) $5 \times 3 =$

(9) $5 \times 9 =$

(10) $5 \times 5 =$

(11) $5 \times 9 =$

(12) $5 \times 3 =$

(13) $5 \times 1 =$

(14) $5 \times 4 =$

(15) $5 \times 10 =$

(16) $5 \times 5 =$

(17) $5 \times 7 =$

(18) $5 \times 2 =$

(19) $5 \times 8 =$

(20) $5 \times 6 =$

Multiplication 5
5×1 to 5×10

Name

Date

■ Multiply the numbers below.

(1) $5 \times 7 =$

(2) $5 \times 3 =$

(3) $5 \times 6 =$

(4) $5 \times 1 =$

(5) $5 \times 10 =$

(6) $5 \times 5 =$

(7) $5 \times 9 =$

(8) $5 \times 4 =$

(9) $5 \times 2 =$

(10) $5 \times 8 =$

(11) $5 \times 2 =$

(12) $5 \times 5 =$

(13) $5 \times 9 =$

(14) $5 \times 7 =$

(15) $5 \times 3 =$

(16) $5 \times 1 =$

(17) $5 \times 8 =$

(18) $5 \times 6 =$

(19) $5 \times 4 =$

(20) $5 \times 10 =$

■ Multiply the numbers below.

(1) $5 \times 1 =$

(2) $5 \times 8 =$

(3) $5 \times 10 =$

(4) $5 \times 3 =$

(5) $5 \times 6 =$

(6) $5 \times 2 =$

(7) $5 \times 7 =$

(8) $5 \times 4 =$

(9) $5 \times 5 =$

(10) $5 \times 9 =$

(11) $5 \times 4 =$

(12) $5 \times 9 =$

(13) $5 \times 1 =$

(14) $5 \times 5 =$

(15) $5 \times 10 =$

(16) $5 \times 6 =$

(17) $5 \times 2 =$

(18) $5 \times 8 =$

(19) $5 \times 3 =$

(20) $5 \times 7 =$

Name

Date

■ Multiply the numbers below.

(1) $4 \times 1 =$

(2) $4 \times 2 =$

(3) $4 \times 3 =$

(4) $4 \times 4 =$

(5) $4 \times 5 =$

(6) $4 \times 6 =$

(7) $4 \times 7 =$

(8) $4 \times 8 =$

(9) $4 \times 9 =$

(10) $4 \times 10 =$

(11) $5 \times 1 =$

(12) $5 \times 2 =$

(13) $5 \times 3 =$

(14) $5 \times 4 =$

(15) $5 \times 5 =$

(16) $5 \times 6 =$

(17) $5 \times 7 =$

(18) $5 \times 8 =$

(19) $5 \times 9 =$

(20) $5 \times 10 =$

Multiplication 4, 5

■ Multiply the numbers below.

(1) $4 \times 4 =$

(2) $4 \times 7 =$

(3) $4 \times 10 =$

(4) $4 \times 2 =$

(5) $4 \times 6 =$

(6) $4 \times 1 =$

(7) $4 \times 8 =$

(8) $4 \times 3 =$

(9) $4 \times 9 =$

(10) $4 \times 5 =$

(11) $5 \times 4 =$

(12) $5 \times 9 =$

(13) $5 \times 1 =$

(14) $5 \times 5 =$

(15) $5 \times 10 =$

(16) $5 \times 6 =$

(17) $5 \times 2 =$

(18) $5 \times 8 =$

(19) $5 \times 3 =$

(20) $5 \times 7 =$

Name

Date

■ Multiply the numbers below.

(1) $4 \times 3 =$

(2) $5 \times 7 =$

(3) $4 \times 9 =$

(4) $5 \times 4 =$

(5) $4 \times 6 =$

(6) $5 \times 10 =$

(7) $4 \times 1 =$

(8) $5 \times 8 =$

(9) $4 \times 2 =$

(10) $5 \times 5 =$

(11) $5 \times 2 =$

(12) $4 \times 8 =$

(13) $5 \times 6 =$

(14) $4 \times 10 =$

(15) $5 \times 9 =$

(16) $4 \times 5 =$

(17) $5 \times 3 =$

(18) $4 \times 7 =$

(19) $5 \times 1 =$

(20) $4 \times 4 =$

Multiplication 4, 5

■ Multiply the numbers below.

(1) $5 \times 9 =$ (11) $4 \times 10 =$

(2) $4 \times 7 =$ (12) $5 \times 3 =$

(3) $5 \times 5 =$ (13) $4 \times 1 =$

(4) $4 \times 6 =$ (14) $5 \times 8 =$

(5) $5 \times 1 =$ (15) $4 \times 5 =$

(6) $4 \times 8 =$ (16) $5 \times 6 =$

(7) $5 \times 10 =$ (17) $4 \times 2 =$

(8) $4 \times 3 =$ (18) $5 \times 4 =$

(9) $5 \times 2 =$ (19) $4 \times 9 =$

(10) $4 \times 4 =$ (20) $5 \times 7 =$

Review
Multiplication 1, 2, 3

■ Multiply the numbers below.

(1) $1 \times 3 =$

(2) $2 \times 7 =$

(3) $3 \times 9 =$

(4) $1 \times 4 =$

(5) $2 \times 6 =$

(6) $3 \times 10 =$

(7) $1 \times 1 =$

(8) $2 \times 8 =$

(9) $3 \times 2 =$

(10) $1 \times 5 =$

(11) $2 \times 2 =$

(12) $3 \times 3 =$

(13) $1 \times 6 =$

(14) $2 \times 10 =$

(15) $3 \times 5 =$

(16) $1 \times 9 =$

(17) $2 \times 4 =$

(18) $3 \times 7 =$

(19) $1 \times 8 =$

(20) $2 \times 1 =$

Multiplication 1, 2, 3

■ Multiply the numbers below.

(1) 3 × 1 =

(2) 1 × 2 =

(3) 2 × 9 =

(4) 3 × 6 =

(5) 1 × 10 =

(6) 2 × 5 =

(7) 3 × 8 =

(8) 1 × 7 =

(9) 2 × 3 =

(10) 3 × 4 =

(11) 3 × 10 =

(12) 2 × 3 =

(13) 1 × 1 =

(14) 3 × 8 =

(15) 2 × 5 =

(16) 3 × 6 =

(17) 1 × 2 =

(18) 2 × 4 =

(19) 3 × 9 =

(20) 2 × 7 =

Name

Date

■ Multiply the numbers below.

(1) $2 \times 3 =$

(2) $3 \times 7 =$

(3) $4 \times 9 =$

(4) $2 \times 4 =$

(5) $3 \times 6 =$

(6) $4 \times 10 =$

(7) $2 \times 1 =$

(8) $3 \times 8 =$

(9) $4 \times 2 =$

(10) $2 \times 5 =$

(11) $3 \times 2 =$

(12) $4 \times 3 =$

(13) $2 \times 6 =$

(14) $3 \times 10 =$

(15) $4 \times 5 =$

(16) $2 \times 9 =$

(17) $3 \times 4 =$

(18) $4 \times 7 =$

(19) $2 \times 8 =$

(20) $3 \times 1 =$

Multiplication 2, 3, 4

■ Multiply the numbers below.

(1) $4 \times 1 =$

(2) $2 \times 2 =$

(3) $3 \times 9 =$

(4) $4 \times 6 =$

(5) $2 \times 10 =$

(6) $3 \times 5 =$

(7) $4 \times 8 =$

(8) $2 \times 7 =$

(9) $3 \times 3 =$

(10) $4 \times 4 =$

(11) $4 \times 10 =$

(12) $3 \times 3 =$

(13) $2 \times 1 =$

(14) $4 \times 8 =$

(15) $3 \times 5 =$

(16) $4 \times 6 =$

(17) $2 \times 2 =$

(18) $3 \times 4 =$

(19) $4 \times 9 =$

(20) $3 \times 7 =$

38

Review
Multiplication 3, 4, 5

■ Multiply the numbers below.

(1) $3 \times 3 =$

(2) $4 \times 7 =$

(3) $5 \times 9 =$

(4) $3 \times 4 =$

(5) $4 \times 6 =$

(6) $5 \times 10 =$

(7) $3 \times 1 =$

(8) $4 \times 8 =$

(9) $5 \times 2 =$

(10) $3 \times 5 =$

(11) $4 \times 2 =$

(12) $5 \times 3 =$

(13) $3 \times 6 =$

(14) $4 \times 10 =$

(15) $5 \times 5 =$

(16) $3 \times 9 =$

(17) $4 \times 4 =$

(18) $5 \times 7 =$

(19) $3 \times 8 =$

(20) $4 \times 1 =$

Multiplication 3, 4, 5

■ Multiply the numbers below.

(1) $5 \times 1 =$

(2) $3 \times 2 =$

(3) $4 \times 9 =$

(4) $5 \times 6 =$

(5) $3 \times 10 =$

(6) $4 \times 5 =$

(7) $5 \times 8 =$

(8) $3 \times 7 =$

(9) $4 \times 3 =$

(10) $5 \times 4 =$

(11) $5 \times 10 =$

(12) $4 \times 3 =$

(13) $3 \times 1 =$

(14) $5 \times 8 =$

(15) $4 \times 5 =$

(16) $5 \times 6 =$

(17) $3 \times 2 =$

(18) $4 \times 4 =$

(19) $5 \times 9 =$

(20) $4 \times 7 =$

39

Review
Multiplication 1 to 5

Name

Date

■ Multiply the numbers below.

(1) $1 \times 3 =$

(2) $2 \times 7 =$

(3) $3 \times 9 =$

(4) $4 \times 4 =$

(5) $5 \times 6 =$

(6) $4 \times 8 =$

(7) $1 \times 5 =$

(8) $2 \times 10 =$

(9) $5 \times 2 =$

(10) $3 \times 8 =$

(11) $3 \times 2 =$

(12) $4 \times 3 =$

(13) $5 \times 9 =$

(14) $1 \times 10 =$

(15) $2 \times 5 =$

(16) $4 \times 9 =$

(17) $5 \times 4 =$

(18) $1 \times 7 =$

(19) $2 \times 8 =$

(20) $3 \times 1 =$

Multiplication I to 5

■ Multiply the numbers below.

(1) 5 × 1 =

(2) 1 × 2 =

(3) 2 × 4 =

(4) 3 × 6 =

(5) 4 × 10 =

(6) 1 × 6 =

(7) 2 × 8 =

(8) 3 × 7 =

(9) 4 × 3 =

(10) 5 × 4 =

(11) 2 × 10 =

(12) 3 × 2 =

(13) 4 × 1 =

(14) 5 × 8 =

(15) 1 × 5 =

(16) 3 × 4 =

(17) 4 × 2 =

(18) 5 × 3 =

(19) 1 × 9 =

(20) 2 × 7 =

Name

Date

Multiply the numbers below.

(1) $4 \times 2 =$

(2) $1 \times 7 =$

(3) $3 \times 9 =$

(4) $5 \times 4 =$

(5) $2 \times 6 =$

(6) $3 \times 10 =$

(7) $1 \times 1 =$

(8) $4 \times 7 =$

(9) $2 \times 2 =$

(10) $5 \times 5 =$

(11) $5 \times 2 =$

(12) $2 \times 3 =$

(13) $4 \times 6 =$

(14) $1 \times 10 =$

(15) $3 \times 5 =$

(16) $2 \times 9 =$

(17) $1 \times 4 =$

(18) $5 \times 7 =$

(19) $4 \times 8 =$

(20) $3 \times 1 =$

Multiplication 1 to 5

■ Multiply the numbers below.

(1) $1 \times 1 =$

(2) $3 \times 2 =$

(3) $5 \times 9 =$

(4) $2 \times 6 =$

(5) $4 \times 10 =$

(6) $2 \times 1 =$

(7) $5 \times 8 =$

(8) $3 \times 7 =$

(9) $1 \times 3 =$

(10) $4 \times 5 =$

(11) $5 \times 10 =$

(12) $3 \times 3 =$

(13) $4 \times 1 =$

(14) $1 \times 8 =$

(15) $2 \times 5 =$

(16) $3 \times 6 =$

(17) $1 \times 2 =$

(18) $4 \times 4 =$

(19) $2 \times 9 =$

(20) $5 \times 7 =$

Certificate of Achievement

is hereby congratulated on completing

My Book of Simple Multiplication

Presented on _____ , 20___

_____
Parent or Guardian

$5 \times 5 = 25$